PRINCESS DIANA

The Tragic Fate of the Nation's Sweetheart

Written by Audrey Schul
Translated by Emma Hanna

DIANA, PRINCESS OF WALES

KEY INFORMATION

- **Born:** 1 July 1961 in Sandringham (Norfolk, United Kingdom).
- **Died:** 31 August 1997 in Paris (France).
- **Main achievements:**
  - First wife of Charles, Prince of Wales (born in 1948), with whom she had two children: Prince William (born in 1982) and Prince Harry (born in 1984), heirs to the British throne.
  - Modernising the British royal family's image.
  - Changing public opinion about AIDS.
  - Increasing public awareness worldwide about the dangers of landmines.

INTRODUCTION

> "Goodbye England's rose
> May you ever grow in our hearts..."

The words of the song *Candle in the Wind* by Elton John (British singer, pianist and composer, born in 1947) still seem to echo through Westminster Abbey ever since he sang them there in honour of his friend Diana, Princess of Wales, during her funeral service in 1997.

Lady Di, as she is sometimes known, was without a doubt one of the best-known princesses of the 20th century. She was born into an aristocratic family as Diana Spencer, and when she was 19, she married the heir to the British throne, Prince Charles. However, their seemingly fairy-tale union soon turned sour, and their marriage was plagued with adultery and jealousy on both sides, eventually leading to their divorce 15 years later in 1996. Although their married life had already been the subject of extensive media attention, the royal couple's separation was the centre of a veritable media storm. Diana came to be seen as a celebrity, and the British public lapped up the newspaper articles, magazine photo spreads and documentaries that mapped out the finest details of her everyday life.

As well as gaining this cult media following, she was a prominent supporter of a variety of humanitarian causes, notably the eradication of landmines and the fight against AIDS, and she did not hesitate to challenge the public's preconceived notions and prejudices about the disease.

On 31 August 1997, Diana and her new paramour were involved in a fatal car crash in the Pont de l'Alma tunnel in Paris. This tragedy left the British public reeling, and triggered an immediate outpouring of tributes to the late princess. She remains beloved in the mind and memory of the British people today.

BIOGRAPHY

Princess Diana in 1982.

BORN TO BE A LADY

Diana Frances Spencer was born on 1 July 1961 in Sandringham, Norfolk. Her family was part of the British aristocracy, as her parents were Edward John Spencer, Viscount Althorp (1924-1992), and his first wife Frances Burke-Roche (1936-2004). Diana was the fourth of five children, and she grew up at Park House with her older sisters Sarah (born in 1955) and Jane (born in 1957) and her younger brother Charles (born in 1964). Her other brother, John (1960-1960), died in infancy, the year before Diana was born.

A ROYAL DWELLING

Park House, the estate where Diana was born and raised, actually belongs to the British royal family. It was rented from the Queen for many years by her maternal grandparents, and later by her parents, and is located beside Sandringham House, the enormous private royal holiday home.

When Diana was seven years old, her parents decided to separate, and they divorced in 1969.

When Diana's paternal grandfather Albert Spencer (1892-1975) died in 1975, her father inherited the title of Earl Spencer, and from then on his daughter became known as Lady Diana. A year later, Earl Spencer married his second wife, Raine McCorquodale (1929-2016), who is the eldest daughter of the famous novelist Barbara Cartland (1901-2000). The family then moved from Park House to the family home of Althorp in Northampton.

| Barbara Cartland in 1987.

Barbara Cartland was a rather eccentric figure who always dressed in shades of pastel, particularly candy pink, and was the author of more than 700 books. Her romance novels have sold around 750 million copies.

EDUCATION AND CAREER

Diana initially attended Silfield Private School in Gayton, Norfolk, but left at the age of nine to enrol at Riddlesworth Hall. She then joined her two sisters at West Heath Girls' School in Sevenoaks, Kent.

As a teenager, she displayed an uncommon talent for music, and proved a gifted pianist. Her dream was to become a prima ballerina. In 1977, when she was 16, she attended the Institut Alpin Videmanette, a private finishing school for the daughters of aristocratic families located in Rougemont, Switzerland. She returned to London to live with her mother Frances in 1978, and began taking on a variety of part-time jobs. She eventually found a job as a nanny for an American family and also worked as a kindergarten teacher at the Young England School in Pimlico. When she turned 18, her mother bought her a flat, where she lived until she embarked on her new life as a princess.

LIFE AS A PRINCESS

At the age of 19, Diana's life was turned upside down. The young woman met the Prince of Wales for the first time in November 1977, at which point he was dating her older sister Sarah. The official story goes that they next saw each other three years later during a polo match in summer 1980. According to the press, this encounter was a real case of love at first sight.

However, a closer look at the history linking the two families reveals that several of Diana's older relatives were well acquainted with the royal family: her maternal grandmother, Lady Fermoy (1908-1993), was one of the Queen Mother's (1900-2002) favourite ladies-in-waiting – the Queen Mother being Prince Charles's grandmother. The future Princess of Wales also just so happened to be of aristocratic descent and single, and it does not take much of a leap of the imagination to wonder if the royal family had always had their eye on Diana Spencer, an unassuming, pretty young girl from an aristocratic family, when they began thinking seriously about Prince Charles's marriage prospects. Was it really love at first sight, or simply a well-staged act? Today, it seems clear that it was the latter, although this has never been officially confirmed.

Charles introduced his girlfriend to his family during a weekend at Balmoral (royal residence in Scotland) in November 1980. Their engagement was initially kept secret before being officially announced on 24 February 1981, and their wedding was held a few months later, on 29 July, in St Paul's Cathedral in London. Through this marriage, Diana became Her Royal Highness The Princess of Wales and Countess of Chester, Duchess of Cornwall, Duchess of Rothesay, Countess of Carrick, Baroness of Renfrew, Lady of the Isles and Princess of Scotland. She kept these titles until her divorce.

Did you know?

The royal wedding was considered the marriage of the century. It was broadcast worldwide on television, and was watched by nearly 750 million viewers. Diana's wedding dress is probably one of the most famous in history, particularly due to its eight-metre train, while her engagement ring featured 14 solitaire diamonds surrounding a sapphire set in white gold. This would later be the ring worn by another young royal bride-to-be, Catherine Middleton.

After the wedding, the couple began carrying out their royal duties together, and the following year, on 21 June 1982, the princess gave birth to William, her first child and the future heir to the throne. She had a second child named Henry (nicknamed Harry) two years later on 15 September 1984.

| The Prince and Princess of Wales with the President and First Lady of the United States, Ronald Reagan and his wife Nancy.

FROM FAIRY TALE TO TRAGEDY

Sadly, it was not long before cracks started to show in this happy façade. The rules and demands of royal life soon took a hefty toll on Diana's health, and she developed depression and bulimia. The royal couple's relationship faced a series of challenges throughout the 1980s, and since the British royal family receives the most media attention of any European monarchy, their marital difficulties soon became media fodder. Even international newspapers ran stories about them, most of which were sensationalised scandals. Diana and Charles began waging a vicious war on each other, in which jibes and accusations of infidelity were constantly being flung back and forth.

It is certainly true that Charles displayed interest in another woman, namely Camilla Parker Bowles (born Camilla Shand in 1947), whom he had met several years earlier. Camilla had been judged too low-born and forthright to be included on the list of potential brides for the Prince of Wales. Similarly, the evidence suggests that Diana also had extra-marital affairs during this time.

The Queen once referred to 1992 as *annus horribilis*, given that three of her children separated from their spouses that year. First, her only daughter, Princess Anne (born in 1950), announced that she was separating from her husband Mark Philips (born in 1948). This was followed by the monarch's second son Andrew, Prince of York (born in 1960) ending his marriage to Sarah Ferguson (born in 1959), whom he had married in 1986. Finally, Charles and Diana officially announced that they were separating on 9 December, sending the media into a veritable frenzy due to Diana's celebrity status. Their divorce was finalised in 1996, meaning that Diana lost her title of Her Royal Highness, but she remained a member of the royal family as the mother of the future heirs to the throne. She kept her title of the Princess of Wales as a purely honorific title.

DID YOU KNOW?

In a year beset with romantic drama, another crisis befell a symbol of British royalty itself when a section of Windsor Castle caught fire. The historian Jean des Cars (born in 1943), who specialises in the history of European royal families, viewed it as a highly symbolic tragedy, saying: "When Windsor burns, it is the monarchy that is consumed"[1] (2012: 425).

The fire blazed through Windsor Castle during the night of 19 November and into

---

1. This quotation has been translated by 50Minutes.com.

the morning of 20 November 1992. It took no fewer than 15 hours to douse the flames, and the building was left devastated: several rooms (including some which were incredibly old) and sections of precious ornamentation were reduced to ash. However, thousands of pieces of artwork and part of the library were saved.

Significant repair work was carried out, and was completed in November 1997. In fact, these renovations turned out to be a blessing in disguise, as they involved a significant degree of archaeological study, which led to a better understanding of the history and origins of Windsor Castle.

A TRAGIC FATE

Despite her divorce and the end of her relationship with the heir to the British throne, Diana never escaped the media's feverish gaze. She was hounded by the press at every step, and details about her private life often made their way onto the front pages of the tabloids.

In July 1997, Diana began a romantic relationship with Dodi Fayed (1955-1997), the son of an Egyptian billionaire. However, this new romance never had a chance to bloom. On 31 August, Dodi and Diana were travelling through Paris in a fresh attempt to escape from the paparazzi when the car they were travelling in crashed into one of the pillars supporting the Pont de l'Alma tunnel. Dodi Fayed and the driver were killed on impact, and Diana died a few hours later at the Pitié-Salpêtrière Hospital in Paris. Her funeral was held on 6 September 1997 in Westminster Abbey, and she was buried on the Althorp estate on a small island surrounded by a lake known as The Round Oval.

Princess Diana's memory lives on in the minds of the people of the United Kingdom, who often affectionately refer to her as "the people's princess".

SOCIAL AND POLITICAL CONTEXT

DARK DAYS FOR BRITAIN

| Official portrait of Margaret Thatcher.

The history of the United Kingdom has been shaped by a series of influential women. Although Diana was certainly one of the most iconic figures of the 1980s and 1990s, she shared the spotlight with another British woman: Margaret Thatcher (1925-2013).

"The Iron Lady", as she was often nicknamed, was elected Prime Minister of the United Kingdom in 1979, becoming the first woman to be appointed leader of a European government. Her rise to power marked a turning point in politics, as her premiership was characterised by the many radical reforms she implemented.

Her main priorities were to drive inflation down, cut taxes, privatise public companies, limit the influence wielded by trade unions and reduce state intervention in the economy. These policies led to difficult times for the British public: industrial production plummeted and unemployment skyrocketed. Her first term as Prime Minister proved difficult, as the government waited for these reforms to bear fruit, and widespread discontentment rippled through British society.

On 2 April 1982, the Falklands War broke out when the Falkland Islands, which are officially classified as British overseas territories, were invaded by Argentina, which claimed them as part of its own territory. The conflict ended with a British victory two months later on 14 June 1982. Many British citizens felt that some of Britain's former glory had been restored, which boosted Thatcher's popularity and meant that she was re-elected for a second term in 1983, which gave her policies fresh impetus.

She soon faced growing opposition from the trade unions. Following the government's decision to close a number of state-owned mines which had been deemed unprofitable, British miners went on strike for a year, from 1984 to 1985. However, the government remained steadfast, and the defeated unions were left severely weakened by the end of the protests. Although productivity began to increase, job security was very low and poverty was rampant. When the British economy did begin to recover, it was almost entirely due to the City and the finance sector.

Thatcher was elected for a third and final term in 1987. After implementing a highly unpopular new taxation system known as the poll tax in 1990, which replaced the previous housing tax system, support for Thatcher's monetary policies began to dwindle, and she announced her retirement from government in November 1990.

DID YOU KNOW?

Thatcher held the post of Prime Minister of the United Kingdom for longer than any previous occupant of the position since 1868.

LIFE IN THE PUBLIC EYE

Of all the societal factors which influenced Princess Diana's story, the ever-growing role of the media and the royal family's increasing proximity to their subjects are probably the most significant.

The British royal family is undeniably still one of the most popular monarchies both in Europe and worldwide. British citizens regard their sovereigns with a certain degree of fascination, and the monarchy is a symbol of both tradition and unity. The royals' lives are filled with just as many joys and dramas as anyone else's, but their reactions to the circumstances they find themselves in are much more visible, and are capable of delighting and shocking the public in equal measure. This means that public opinion can be fickle: favourable one moment, and hostile the next. After 60 years on the throne, Queen Elizabeth II (born in 1926) knows this better than most. Following the various dramas that rocked Buckingham Palace in 1992, she once described the year as an *annus horribilis*. However, one man's loss is another man's profit, and the press certainly raked in a healthy profit from the scandals, as the British royal family has always been one of its favourite subjects. Unsurprisingly, these two parties have had a tumultuous relationship for many years as a result.

After the death of her father, King George VI, on 6 February 1952, Princess Elizabeth acceded to the British throne and became Head of the Commonwealth at the age of 26. One year later, on 2 June 1953, she was crowned Queen of the

United Kingdom in Westminster Abbey, becoming the last British monarch to be crowned in the 20th century. This historic event was broadcast live on television in five countries: the United Kingdom, France, Belgium, the Netherlands and Germany, which helped pave the way to make Elizabeth the most frequently photographed monarch of the period, as well as the most popular with the media. She and her family often made the headlines, particularly during times of turmoil.

This image of a fairy-tale royal family may have boosted the country's stability, but a royal title does not grant its holder immunity from the trials and tribulations of life. The royal family's supposedly idyllic life would soon be thrown into turmoil, starting with the media interest surrounding the romantic relationships of Elizabeth's younger sister Margaret (1930-2002). Her personal life frequently made the headlines, which somewhat diminished the royal family's standing in the eyes of the public. The Queen had not yet learned the dangers of underestimating how public the royal family's private lives could be.

In 1977, the Queen celebrated the Silver Jubilee (25th anniversary) of her reign. The festivities held in her honour were a resounding success and reaffirmed her popularity. Despite this, the media was gaining such an unprecedented level of influence that it was becoming almost inescapable. While the members of the royal family had once been seen as symbols of the nation, they were now becoming part of an international celebrity class, though they still retained a certain aura of privilege.

This trend only intensified when Diana arrived on the scene. A beautiful young woman with a close bond with the people, unhappily trapped in her roles of princess and wife, was the perfect story for the media to sell. Her rocky relationships with her husband and step-mother were sensationalised by the press, and the British public felt obliged to weigh in on the drama. In fact, the public generally sided with Diana, as they felt great fondness for her, whereas the Windsors were generally seen as overly aloof. The revelations concerning Charles's infidelity with Camilla only increased Diana's popularity, while the royal family's reputation became increasingly tarnished.

Although the British public eagerly lapped up all the news of these scandals, they also served to discredit the monarchy's standing as an institution that is supposed to represent stability and tradition.

KEY MOMENTS

THE MARRIAGE OF THE CENTURY

The young Diana Spencer was a shy, unassuming girl; there were no clues that hinted at her future position in one of the most prominent royal families of the 20th century. She was born into an aristocratic family which boasted several ancestors who had worked for the British Crown, and she officially met her future husband for the first time in 1977.

At that time, the royal family was growing increasingly concerned about the relationship that the Crown Prince, who at that time was 32 years old, had started with a married woman, Camilla Parker Bowles. In an attempt to ensure that the prince married someone more appropriate to his rank, the Queen sought out a more suitable candidate. Enter Diana, a young woman from an aristocratic family who was aged 19 at the time. Although the press painted their first encounter as love at first sight, the reality of the situation was rather different. The Spencers were no strangers to the royal family: Diana's father had previously served as a squire to the Queen, who was also her younger brother's godmother. In other words, Charles and Diana would probably have met each other on several previous occasions. In spite of Camilla and Charles's closeness, Diana accepted when Charles proposed to her in 1981.

Their marriage was of a certain historical importance, because the previous wedding of a Prince of Wales took place in 1863 (the marriage of the future King Edward VII, 1841-1910, to Alexandra of Denmark, 1844-1925). Public and media excitement surrounding the wedding soon reached fever pitch. The ceremony took place in St Paul's Cathedral in London, instead of the traditional location of Westminster Abbey, and was attended by a staggering 2700 guests. It was broadcast on 90 different television channels, meaning that it was also watched by an additional 750 million viewers throughout the world. Their union, which was touted as the "marriage of the century" (as was their son William's wedding the following century), swept the House of Windsor into the modern age.

| Back cover of the record sleeve for the recording of the marriage ceremony, produced by the BBC.

SEPARATION AND DIVORCE IN THE SPOTLIGHT

Royal life soon proved difficult for Diana. She struggled to find her place in spite of her best efforts, and her health proved equally fragile, as she suffered from bulimia and periods of depression. On top of that, her relationship with Charles was already coming under strain.

However, these difficulties took a back seat for a time during the princess's first pregnancy. The couple's first child, Prince William, was born on 23 June 1982, followed by Prince Harry two years later on 15 September 1984. Diana had a very close relationship with her children, and took an active role in their upbringing, only deferring to her husband or to other members of the royal family on rare occasions. In a break with convention and in the face of criticism, she personally selected their nanny and their schools, as well as taking them with her when carrying out her royal duties.

In spite of the happiness they found through the birth of their sons, the couple's relationship continued to flounder. The Prince of Wales reconnected with Camilla in 1987, after which point his marriage to Diana became little more than a façade. They each hurled accusations of adultery at the other: Charles with Camilla, and Diana with James Hewitt (born in 1958). This turmoil was a veritable feast for the media, which took great delight in captivating the public with each and every detail of the successive scandals. An increasing number of books and articles on the subject were published, and one particular book was astonishingly successful: *Diana, Her True Story* by Andrew Morton (born in 1953). In it, the princess painted herself as the wife of a cheating husband who received absolutely no support from the royal family. She also talked about her struggles with bulimia, her loneliness and her previous suicide attempts. These revelations sent shockwaves rippling through British society. Diana's revealing comments prompted the Queen and her husband to take Charles's side, while public opinion came down firmly in favour of the victimised princess.

On 9 December 1992, the Prime Minister John Major (born in 1943) announced the couple's official separation, while emphasising the fact that it was not a divorce. They continued to raise their children together, and also appeared together in certain national or familial contexts. However, the scandals continued to pour forth: a private conversation between Charles and Camilla dating from 1989 was leaked to the press, followed by private photographs of Diana and then an interview between the princess and the BBC in which she lamented her marital woes. During the interview, she stated that she did not want to get a divorce and that she had no desire to rule in an official capacity, but she also expressed doubt over Charles's ability to rule.

This was the final straw. The monarchy had had enough of the couple's endless squabbles, which it now saw as a real threat to its own standing, and the Queen herself encouraged her son and daughter-in-law to start divorce proceedings. Their divorce was finalised on 28 August 1996, after which both parents continued to play an active role in the upbringing of William and Harry (who were 15 and 12 at that time, respectively). Diana kept her offices at St James's Palace and was permitted to continue living at Kensington Palace. She also kept her title of Princess of Wales, but was no longer styled Her Royal Highness.

In accordance with long-standing tradition, the princes and princesses of the British royal family who are styled Their Royal Highness must give up their own family name, and their surname officially becomes Mountbatten-Windsor.

King George V chose the new name of the royal house in 1917, changing it from Saxe-Cobourg and Gotha to Windsor. The British monarch's decision was motivated by the desire to distance himself from his German ancestry in the wake of the First World War (1914-1918), and he therefore changed his German-sounding family name to a more typically English name: specifically Windsor, the name of one of the most iconic royal residences.

In 1960, Queen Elizabeth II and her husband Prince Philip (born in 1921) also decided to create a family name that would be used by their direct descendants. This name is a composite of the name of the royal family – which did not change – and Mountbatten, Philip's original family name.

In spite of their divorce, the glamour surrounding the lives of Prince Charles and his ex-wife never diminished. The press's interest in Diana's personal life showed no signs of abating, and she became one of the most photographed women in the world. The constant media frenzy surrounding Diana's new lovers was deemed intolerable by the Queen, who accused her former daughter-in-law of taking pleasure in provoking the royal family as a form of revenge.

"ROCK 'N' ROYALTY"

On 24 February 1981, when Prince Charles officially announced his engagement to Lady Diana Spencer, the young couple were engulfed in an unprecedented whirlwind of media and public interest. A few months later, the whole world was invited to watch their wedding on television, and one particular moment captured the public imagination: the famous, never-before-seen kiss shared by the newlywed couple on the balcony of Buckingham Palace! From that moment on, the British public's fascination with the royal couple only grew, as did the constant clamour for more gossip about their lives.

The 1980s were also a time of cultural shift, and introduced sweeping changes in terms of music and fashion. Style and appearance became more important than ever before, and the media took full advantage of this new trend, as can be seen in the magazines and advertising campaigns from that time.

Diana, who was already a favourite target of the paparazzi, decided to break with royal convention and adopted a more chic, modern style. The result was sensational: she became a style icon, and brought a new sense of luxury to the fashion world. Her outfits, which were constantly analysed and commented on by the media, became the embodiment of British style for the rest of the world, which *Vogue* magazine dubbed "rock 'n' royalty".

| Princess Diana on the cover of *Vogue* in May 1993.

The princess fitted in perfectly during a decade when extravagant fashion and music were used as ways of trying to drive away the bad times, or at least to conceal them. When the fairy-tale existence she had been promised turned out to be nothing more than smoke and mirrors, Diana used the tools at her disposal in the period she was living in to try to protect her gentle soul as best she could.

Over time, as Diana continued to defy the rules, she made her own mark through her charisma and her philanthropy. She was seen as a modern royal, and her love for her children and the failure of her marriage contributed to the public's perception of her as a normal person, in spite of her rank. Many people's difficulties were alleviated because of Diana's efforts, and her goodwill, her elegance and her determination combined to make her an icon of modernity, fashion and kindness.

| Photo of the princess printed in the magazine *Vanity Fair.*

TRYING TIMES

| Princess Diana with Mother Teresa.

Diana made numerous public appearances in her capacity as a royal princess, particularly to schools and hospitals, as a way of supporting a variety of charitable organisations. As a result, she became the president of many different charities working with sick children, the homeless or drug addicts. She travelled all over the world to fulfil her commitments, and had the chance to meet some well-known representatives of these organisations. In 1992, Diana visited a hospital in Calcutta, India where she met Mother Teresa (1910-1997), with whom she struck up a friendship that would last until her death.

During a short stay in Russia in 1995, where she was visiting a children's hospital, the princess was awarded the prestigious International Leonardo Prize, which is awarded to individuals and sponsors who have made an exceptional contribution to the field of art, medicine or sport.

Princess Diana's philanthropic activities went far beyond what was expected of her as a royal. Wracked with loneliness in private, she sought to forget her own problems by helping those whose suffering was greater. Her humanitarian efforts breathed new life into the monarchy's involvement with charitable organisations, which had previously tended to be much more impersonal in nature. The princess's compassion proved her greatest weapon, as it greatly strengthened her position within the royal family.

Of course, she was not the first royal to get involved with charitable causes, but she was certainly the first to harness her own fame so effectively as a means of supporting them, as she did not hesitate to turn the same media that broadcast the details of her personal life for everyone to see and hear to her own advantage in order to bring the causes closest to her heart to greater public attention. Furthermore, Diana's charity work went beyond raising awareness: she got involved on the ground, even when it posed a danger to her own safety, such as her trip to Angola to combat the dangers of landmines. For Diana, the photos and stories that resulted from each humanitarian or charitable campaign she participated in represented a way of leveraging her own fame for the benefit of the causes she felt strongly about.

Continuing her charity work remained a priority for Diana even after her divorce from Prince Charles, although she reduced the number of charities she supported so that she could focus her efforts on a handful of causes that lay particularly close to her heart, especially the fights against AIDS and landmines.

AIDS

During the 1980s, a number of deadly diseases began appearing or evolving, including AIDS (acquired immune deficiency syndrome). The epidemic began in 1981, when the disease began appearing in a number of American cities. Through exhaustive scientific research, doctors were able to identify the virus that caused the disease, and researchers named it "human immunodeficiency virus" (HIV) in 1986. Over time, the epidemic spread and soon became a pandemic. As awareness of the gravity of the situation grew, the General Assembly of the United Nations met on 26 October 1987 to call on all of its member states to combat the spread of AIDS. The UN also established a programme known as UNAIDS to fight the disease.

Many celebrities, including Princess Diana, decided to help and support this cause. In 1989, Diana participated in the opening ceremony of Landmark Aids Centre in South London, and she also famously hugged a young girl who was HIV-positive during a visit to Grandma's House, a centre in Washington, D. C. for young victims of the disease.

She played a pivotal role in changing public attitudes towards victims of HIV and AIDS. At that time, many people believed that the virus could be contracted simply by making physical contact with an infected individual. While on a trip to São Paolo in Brazil in 1991, Diana took deliberate steps to combat this stigma by allowing herself to be photographed while holding a young victim of the disease and while shaking hands with infected individuals. These images soon spread around the world, allowing the princess's seemingly inconsequential gesture to increase global consciousness of the isolation that affected individuals had to endure. Once again, Diana had turned the all-seeing eye of the media to her advantage, and increased public sympathy towards victims of AIDS.

These photos also drew the ire of the Queen, who disapproved of her daughter-in-law's involvement with this particular issue. She advised Diana to stick to more "pleasant" causes, which only spurred Diana to throw herself even more wholeheartedly into working with the causes she was passionate about.

In March 1997, just a few months before her death, she travelled to South Africa to meet with President Nelson Mandela (1918-2013) with the aim of collaborating with him in efforts to raise money to help AIDS victims.

Landmines

Another worthy cause that captured the princess's interest was that of landmines. As a patron of The HALO Trust, she met with victims and learned about future landmine removal projects. She also supported a number of awareness campaigns about the many dangers posed by these mines.

THE HALO TRUST

The HALO Trust is an organisation which was founded in 1988 by Colin Mitchell, his wife Susan Mitchell and Guy Willoughby. All three had witnessed the harm caused by landmines and the debris from other explosives in the wake of the Soviet-Afghan War in 1988, and decided to take action to improve the situation. Over time, their mission's scope and impact grew, as did the number of people involved. In 2009, after the civil war in Sri Lanka, humanitarian volunteers successfully destroyed 100 000 anti-personnel landmines, allowing the local population to return to their homes safely. The HALO Trust is currently active in Syria and Ukraine.

In January 1997, she travelled to Angola in south-western Africa. This was another trip that stirred up media attention when she was photographed in a minefield wearing a ballistic helmet and a flak jacket – another image that broke with royal convention.

In August that year, shortly before her death, she visited Bosnia and Herzegovina with the Landmine Survivors Network, focusing on the bodily harm these weapons can cause, particularly to children. These charities aim to raise awareness of the human costs of using these weapons so that their use will eventually be banned worldwide.

Diana's commitment to the fight against AIDS and the fight against the use of landmines bore considerable social and political results.

"GOODBYE ENGLAND'S ROSE"

Despite all of the high points throughout Diana's life, one moment stands above the rest, and will be forever etched into our collective memory: her tragic death on 31 August 1997. The accident happened in Paris during the night of Saturday 30 to Sunday 31 August, in the Pont de l'Alma tunnel. After divorcing Charles, Diana's love life continued to fascinate the media; even the smallest gesture could make the headlines. Furthermore, the Prince of Wales was no longer hiding his relationship with Camilla, leaving the gossip columns spoilt for choice.

In July 1997, the princess embarked on a relationship with Dodi Fayed, the son of Mohamed al-Fayed (born in 1929), an extremely rich Egyptian businessman. The two of them spent July together in Saint-Tropez, along with William and Harry. While the two children re-joined their father at Balmoral House in August, Diana and Dodi remained in each other's company on a romantic cruise along the coasts of Sardinia – although of course they were unable to escape the all-seeing gaze of the paparazzi even there. The couple then took a short trip to the French capital, where they stayed in the Hôtel Ritz, a property owned by Dodi's father. Around midnight, for reasons that remain unclear, the two lovers plus Diana's bodyguard got into a car that was driven by Henri Paul. Shortly afterwards, the car crashed into a tunnel pillar at high speed, killing Fayed and the driver on impact. A gravely injured Diana was taken to Pitié-Salpêtrière Hospital in Paris, and Queen Elizabeth was immediately informed, as was the French President Jacques Chirac (born in 1932). Despite receiving treatment, Diana succumbed to her injuries that night, dying at the age of 36. The Queen was informed immediately.

Tributes poured in both in Britain and around the world as the news broke of this beloved icon's untimely death. Her funeral service was held on 6 September 1997. The grief-stricken British public looked on via television screens across the nation as the princess's coffin was carried to Westminster Abbey, surrounded by Charles, her two sons, Queen Elizabeth and Prince Philip, the Queen Mother and Diana's own brother and sisters. The ceremony was an emotional one, and many of Diana's friends gave speeches in her honour. However, she was buried in Althorp, the Spencer family's ancestral home, far from the media's gaze and the crowds that thronged the streets of London. Princess Diana's remains are buried there to this day, on a small island in the middle of a lake in the park. This resting place was chosen by her brother Lord Spencer in order to ensure that she could be buried privately, in the presence of her children and family members only.

IMPACT

CONSPIRACY THEORIES SURROUNDING HER DEATH

Although the vagaries of fate are the most likely culprit for Princess Diana's tragic death, numerous conspiracy theories about it – many of them farfetched – have nevertheless emerged over the years.

While the authorities quickly concluded that the crash was accidental, the circumstances surrounding it have long been the subject of passionate debate. One theory plays up the role of the swarm of paparazzi that was following the car on motorcycles, but this version of events has been disputed. Another theory asserts that the driver was inebriated, as a handful of witnesses stated that he was drunk before he got behind the wheel. During the course of the inquiry, statements from hotel staff and a variety of blood tests carried out on the driver's body confirmed that he had consumed alcohol and taken medication that evening.

Some people are also sceptical about the very claim that her death was an accident, and suggest that it was a deliberate attack or even a conspiracy. It has been suggested that the princess's actions to combat the dangers of landmines could have proven inconvenient for certain government leaders, and the royal family itself has even been the subject of accusations that Diana was executed on their orders because she was causing too much trouble for them.

Despite the numerous theories that have cropped up and the lack of conclusive evidence, the death was officially ruled accidental. However, Dodi Fayed's father remains convinced that foul play was involved, and a degree of mystery surrounds the crash to this day.

Memorial for Diana and Dodi in Harrods, erected in 1998 by Mohamed Al-Fayed, Dodi's father, then-CEO of the London department store.

TOWARDS A RECONCILIATION WITH THE MEDIA

Diana's tragic death in 1997 was an emotional blow that was felt around the world. The princess's loved ones and the public grieved as one, and tributes and expressions of sympathy from

British citizens flooded in. However, this only served to throw the Crown's silence into starker relief.

The Queen and the rest of the royal family remained silent in the face of their subjects' grief, which was not without consequences. The Queen's cold reaction to the death of a woman that the press was now unanimously heralding as an idol tarnished the monarchy's image considerably. This was the first time the Queen had faced outright hostility from the people since the beginning of her reign. The Queen usually has a knack for accurately perceiving any problems that are troubling her kingdom, so what could have spurred her to act so aloof during such a trying time? It is true that Diana held a special place in the hearts of the British people, which often negatively impacted the Queen's own popularity, although she is held in very high regard nonetheless. However, on this occasion, royal "indifference" soon came to be seen as a betrayal of the people.

In the days that followed, the Queen's messages of compassion and frequent public appearances did nothing to assuage the people's bitterness: it was all seen as too little, too late. Furthermore, the memory of Princess Diana was in no way fading from people's minds: in 1999, the newspaper *The Times* named Diana the number one most important figure of the 20th century, while a survey carried out by the BBC in 2002 placed her third on a list of the 100 most famous British individuals – ahead of the Queen. Stephen Frears (British director, born in 1941) created a vibrant portrayal of this turmoil in his film *The Queen* (2006).

The road to mending public opinion proved long and difficult. In 2002, the death of the Queen Mother, who was seen as a symbol of national unity, along with the Queen's sister Margaret, went some way toward restoring the British people's affection for their monarch.

Confidence in the monarchy finally surged anew in 2011 thanks to one highly-anticipated event: the marriage of Diana and Charles's oldest son, William, to Catherine Middleton (born in 1982) in April 2011. That year, a survey revealed that 76% of the British population supported the Crown. Two billion viewers worldwide watched the wedding on television, an audience which was four times larger than that of Charles and Diana's wedding 30 years previously.

| Crowds gather for the wedding of Kate and William.

The wedding breathed fresh life into the British monarchy, and its popularity surged. Soon afterwards, the birth of their children George, on 22 July 2013, and his sister Charlotte Elizabeth Diana in 2015 heralded a new generation of the monarchy.

CHARLES'S SECOND MARRIAGE

After they met at a polo match in 1971, the bond that quickly grew between Charles and Camilla proved unshakeable, despite their respective first marriages to other people. Naturally, their relationship caused countless scandals throughout Charles's life with Diana, both because of their status as a royal couple and because of Diana's popularity. Camilla divorced her husband in 1995 and Charles and Diana's divorce was finalised in 1996, but it was not until 9 April 2005, 34 years after they first met, that they were finally able to wed.

While Charles kept his title as the Prince of Wales, Camilla, who should have automatically been granted the title of Princess of Wales through marriage, opted instead to be styled Her Royal Highness The Duchess of Cornwall, doubtlessly to prove to the British people that she was not seeking to usurp Diana's place in their hearts. The marriage drew considerable criticism, because many people viewed Camilla as the main culprit for the failure of Charles and Diana's marriage, and therefore despised the idea of her taking

Diana's place. Despite the eight years that separated Diana's death and this second wedding, the British public were still finding it difficult to lay the past to rest. However, while Camilla initially received a frosty reception from the public, time does heal all wounds, and she has been able to gradually win over public opinion in more recent years.

THE NOBEL PEACE PRIZE

In addition to her charisma and kindness, Diana showed tremendous fighting spirit when it came to fighting for the humanitarian causes that lay close to her heart. The many photos that show her shaking hands with AIDS victims played a vital role in the campaigns to raise awareness and sensitivity about the disease.

Her efforts in support of her other major cause, the fight against anti-personnel landmines, also bore considerable fruit: on 3 December 1997, the Ottawa Treaty (also known as the Mine Ban Treaty) was signed, and it entered into effect a year and a half later on 1 March 1999. This was an international disarmament treaty which prohibited the acquisition, production, stockpiling and use of anti-personnel landmines. In homage to her memory, the International Campaign to Ban Landmines (ICBL) received the Nobel Peace Prize a few months after Princess Diana's death.

SUMMARY

- Diana Frances Spencer was born on 1 July 1961 in Park House in Sandringham, Norfolk. She was the youngest daughter of John Spencer, Viscount Althorp, and his first wife, Frances. She grew up with her two sisters, Sarah and Jane, and her younger brother Charles. Another sibling, John, was born a year before Diana in 1960, but died in infancy.
- Upon the death of Diana's paternal grandfather in 1975, her father John Spencer inherited his title, Earl Spencer. Diana then became Lady Diana Spencer, and was often affectionately referred to as "Lady Di", particularly in Europe. One year later in 1976, Earl Spencer married Raine McCorquodale, having divorced Diana's mother in 1968. The Spencer family then moved to Althorp.
- After being educated at Silfield Private School in Gayton (Norfolk), Diana finished her education at the Institut Alpin Videmanette, a finishing school in Switzerland. She then returned to London, where she took on a series

of odd jobs, including acting as a nanny for an American family and as a kindergarten teacher at Young England School in Pimlico.

- Diana met Prince Charles for the first time in 1977. They met again in summer 1980, and a few months later, Diana was invited to the royal family's Scottish residence of Balmoral to meet Charles's family. Their engagement was announced on 24 February 1981 after initially being kept under wraps.
- On 29 July 1981, Diana married the Prince of Wales, the heir to the British throne. Their wedding was held in St Paul's Cathedral in London. Through this marriage, Diana became Her Royal Highness The Princess of Wales and Countess of Chester, Duchess of Cornwall, Duchess of Rothesay, Countess of Carrick, Baroness of Renfrew, Lady of the Isles and Princess of Scotland.
- In 1982, one year after her wedding, the Princess of Wales gave birth to her first child, William, followed by his younger brother Henry, known as Harry, in 1984.
- In addition to the many visits she carried out in an official capacity, Diana was also known for her humanitarian activities as a patron of

various charitable organisations. She was particularly invested in the fight against AIDS and the elimination of anti-personnel landmines.

- Following a turbulent relationship, the royal couple decided to separate in 1992.
- On 28 August 1996, Charles and Diana's divorce was finalised. Diana was no longer styled Her Royal Highness, but retained the title Princess of Wales.
- One year later, Princess Diana died at the age of 36. Her tragic death was caused by a car accident in the Pont de l'Alma tunnel in Paris. Diana's companion Dodi Fayed and the driver of the vehicle also lost their lives in the crash.

We want to hear from you!
Leave a comment on your online library
and share your favourite books on social media!

FURTHER READING

BIBLIOGRAPHY

- Cars, J. (2014) *La saga des grandes dynasties*. Paris: Éditions Perrin.

- Cars, J. (2012) *La saga des reines*. Paris: Éditions Perrin.

- Cars, J. (2011) *La saga des Windsor. De l'Empire britannique au Commonwealth*. Paris: Éditions Perrin.

- Davies, N. (1996) *Diana: The Abandoned Princess*. London: Birch Lane Press.

- Davies, N. (1998) *The Princess Who Changed the World*. London: Blake Publishing.

- (No date) Diana, Princess of Wales. *The Telegraph*. [Online]. [Accessed 13 December 2017]. Available from: <http://www.telegraph.co.uk/news/newstopics/diana>

- Martin, R. G. and Quadruppani, S. (1985). *Charles and Diana*. New York: Putnam Publishing Group.

- (2017) Princess Diana Biography. *Biography.com*. [Online]. [Accessed 13 December 2017]. Available from: <https://www.biography.com/people/princess-diana-9273782>

- (1990) Princess Diana Tours Aids Home For Youngsters. *Deseret News*. [Online]. [Accessed 13 December 2017]. Available from: <https://www.deseretnews.com/article/125531/PRINCESS-DIANA-TOURS-AIDS-HOME-FOR-YOUNGSTERS.html?pg=all>

- Servat, H. and Boulay, C. (1998) *Princesses de légende : Sissi, Astrid, Wallis, Rita, Margaret, Soraya, Ira, Grace, Paola, Diana*. Paris: Albin Michel.

- (No date) The Royal Family name. The Royal Family website. [Online]. [Accessed 13 December 2017]. Available from: <https://www.royal.uk/royal-family-name>

ADDITIONAL SOURCES

- Coward, R. and Mandela, N. (2007) *Diana the Portrait*. London: Andrew McMeels Publishing.

- Graham, T. (1997) *Diana, Princess of Wales: A Tribute*. New York: Weidenfeld and Nicolson.

- Kurz, M. and Gauthey, C. (1997) *Diana: A Princess for the World*. New York: Barnes and Noble.

- Morton, A. (2017) *Diana: Her True Story – In Her Own Words: 25th Anniversary Edition*. London: Michael O'Mara.

- Official website of Althorp, the Spencer family residence: <http://spencerofalthorp.com>

ICONOGRAPHIC SOURCES

- Princess Diana in 1982. Royalty-free reproduction image.

- Barbara Cartland in 1987. Royalty-free reproduction image.

- The Prince and Princess of Wales with the President and First Lady of the United States, Ronald Reagan and his wife Nancy. Royalty-free reproduction image.

- Official portrait of Margaret Thatcher. Royalty-free reproduction image.

- Back cover of the record sleeve for the recording of the marriage ceremony, produced by the BBC. Royalty-free reproduction image.

- Princess Diana on the cover of *Vogue* in May 1993. Royalty-free reproduction image.

- Photo of the princess printed in the magazine *Vanity Fair*. Royalty-free reproduction image.

- Princess Diana with Mother Teresa. Royalty-free reproduction image.

- Memorial for Diana and Dodi in Harrods, erected in 1998 by Mohamed Al-Fayed, Dodi's father, then-CEO of the London department store. Royalty-free reproduction image.

- Crowds gather for the wedding of Kate and William. Royalty-free reproduction image.

FILMS AND DOCUMENTARIES

- *The Queen*. (2006) [Film]. Stephen Frears. Dir. United Kingdom: Pathé.

- *Diana*. (2013) [Film]. Oliver Hirschbiegel. Dir. United Kingdom/France: Entertainment One.

LITERATURE

- Cossé, L. (2011) *An Accident in August*. Trans. Anderson, A. New York: Europa.

- Townsend, S. (1992) *The Queen and I*. London: Penguin.

COMMEMORATIVE BUILDINGS AND OBJECTS

- *Candle in the Wind*, a song composed by Elton John in 1973 in tribute to Marilyn Monroe, which he rewrote in 1997 in tribute to Princess Diana, who was a very close friend of his. The remake was more successful than the original version.

- Commemorative 25 pence coin for the wedding of Charles and Diana (1981).

- Diana, Princess of Wales Memorial Fountain in Hyde Park, London, inaugurated by Queen Elizabeth II.

- Diana, Princess of Wales Memorial Gardens in Regent Centre Gardens, Kirkintilloch (Scotland).

- Diana, Princess of Wales Memorial Playground in Kensington Gardens, London.

- Diana, Princess of Wales Memorial Walk, a circular path linking Kensington Gardens, Green Park, Hyde Park and St James's Park in London.

- Doric-style memorial to Princess Diana in Althorp, Northampton.

- *The Flame of Liberty* in Paris. This monument is a replica of the torch held by the Statue of Liberty, and was a gift to the nation of France from the United States of America symbolising Franco-American friendship. As the sculpture is located near the Place de l'Alma, above the tunnel where the fatal accident took place, it has become an unofficial memorial site for the Princess of Wales.

- The Stables Block, exhibition hall devoted to the history of the Spencer family on the Althorp estate.

Although the editor makes every effort to verify the accuracy of the information published, 50Minutes. com accepts no responsibility for the content of this book.

© 50MINUTES.com, 2018. All rights reserved.

www.50minutes.com

Ebook EAN: 9782808006736

Paperback EAN: 9782808007399

Legal Deposit: D/2017/12603/946

Cover: © Primento

Digital conception by Primento, the digital partner of publishers.